Animals
Animals Animals

Koalas

By Alison Tibbitts and
Alan Roocroft

PUBLISHED BY
Capstone Press
Mankato, Minnesota USA

CIP
LIBRARY OF CONGRESS CATALOGING IN PUBLICATION DATA

Tibbitts, Alison.
 Koalas / by Alison Tibbitts and Alan Roocroft.
   p. cm. -- (Animals, animals, animals)
 Summary: Discusses the physical characteristics, behavior, and life cycle of koalas and their current status as an endangered species.

 ISBN 1-56065-103-2
 1. Koala--Juvenile literature. [1. Koala, 2. Rare animals. 3. Wildlife conservation.] I. Roocroft, Alan. II. Title. III. Series: Tibbitts, Alison. Animals, animals, animals.
 QL737.M384T53 1992
 599.2--dc20

             92-11446
             CIP
             AC

Consultant:
Valerie Thompson, Lead Keeper
Zoological Society of San Diego

Photo Credits:
Alison Tibbitts and Alan Roocroft: Cover, title page, 3, 8, 15, 16, 27, 32, back cover

Ron Garrison, Zoological Society of San Diego: 4, 7, 11, 20, 23

Australian Koala Foundation: 12, 24, 28

Bob Grieser, Los Angeles Times: 19

Capstone Press
P.O. Box 669, Mankato, MN, U.S.A. 56002-0669

Eucalyptus trees grow in south and east Australia. Their branches are full of lush and tender leaves. High up in the forks of these trees sit sleeping mounds of gray fur. The koalas are at home.

These animals go back to **pre-historic time**. Perhaps they have survived so long because their country has no large **predators**. Australia's Katang tribe called them "kaloine" which means "do not drink." From "kaloine" evolved the word "koala."

Such creatures are not bears at all. They are **marsupials**, or **pouched animals**. Marsupials' babies develop in a special way. After birth, they crawl into their mother's pouch to finish growing. Some marsupials are nearly **extinct**. Only those in Australia and a few **species** in Central and South America are left.

Koalas are **arboreal**, which means they live in trees. They eat and sleep over a hundred feet up in the air. Each one has a home range of about fourteen trees. They do prefer some forks in the branches over others. But no one tree is their favorite. Koalas have excellent balance and rarely fall even in windy weather. They are solitary. They do not live in groups. Only a mother and her baby will share a tree.

These creatures have unique bodies. Fluffy hair frames the ears. Extra padding cushions their backs and rumps for sitting comfortably in trees. They have hands and feet, but almost no tail. Their long and woolly fur can be from light to dark charcoal gray. The neck and chest are white.

Koalas cannot see well. Their brown button eyes stare openly. They seem not to blink. The large, leathery nose has a keen sense of smell. Front **incisor** teeth cut leaves for back **molars** to grind. **Fuse-joined** toes on the back feet are handy for grooming their fur.

These animals are well adapted for climbing. Long arms wrap around the tree. Thumbs and first fingers make a circle to grasp branches. Needle-sharp claws cling to the trunk. Strong back legs carry koalas up and down. They can jump several feet from branch to branch. Sometimes, they bail out of a tree without any landing spot in mind.

Twilight and soon after dark are busy times. This is when koalas are likely to move from tree to tree. Although they can run, they spend little time on the ground. They scurry up the tree again to avoid predators.

Koalas sleep eighteen to twenty hours a day because they get tired easily. They eat every few hours. Afterward, they fold their arms across their chests. They lean forward to rest against a branch. They nod off again.

Koalas are picky, picky eaters. They need a little over a pound of eucalyptus leaves every day. However, they sniff each and every leaf before eating it. Only young, tender leaves and shoots will do. Older or tougher leaves are often rejected. Koalas would rather eat nothing at all than take leaves they do not like. The animals receive their water through the leaves.

Communication helps them keep in touch with other koalas nearby. One way they communicate is by marking trees with scent from a gland in the chest. This tells others they have been there. Koalas also make noises to each other. Males have deep, guttural sounds. Female voices are higher pitched. Both make a sort of scream if they are frightened. Loud clicking means anger. Babies grunt in distress if they feel abandoned.

Females are more active and less hungry during breeding season. This is the only time they do not resist male company. A male stays near his females until the babies come. Females raise their young alone. A single baby arrives once a year. Twins are rare because of the mother's small pouch. If a mother has two babies, it is likely she has adopted an orphan.

A baby comes one month after mating. It is pink, blind, deaf. It is the size of a human's thumbnail and weighs under one ounce. It crawls into the pouch and attaches itself to a **teat**. It will remain attached for four months while it grows. Its mother is careful not to bump her pouch during this time.

The baby has developed by the end of six months. It is eight inches long and furry. It now takes short trips out of the pouch. Its mother watches it learn about life through trial and error. She lets it know if it hurts her by mistake.

The baby inspects and nibbles leaves by seven months. Space is getting tight inside the pouch. It pokes its face out of the opening when its mother travels. It leaves the pouch often and returns only when it is sleepy or scared. The baby is becoming too big and heavy for mother to carry in front. She shifts it to her back. It will ride there for another two months.

Koalas are eating only leaves by their first birthday. The time comes for them to find a home range of their own. Going away can be hard. They may complain loudly and stay near their mothers for a while. They have moved to their trees by eighteen months. They will live there and munch leaves for the next ten or more years.

These creatures are among the world's best loved animals. Many hunters tracked them in the past for their soft pelts. The Australian government began to protect them in this century. The United States was the first country to ban importation of their fur.

Now the gentle koalas are in trouble again. They are headed toward becoming an **endangered species**. Many of their eucalyptus trees are being cut down. Humans are moving in and dividing the habitat. "Koala crossing" signs warn drivers not to hit the animals. Only a few zoos are able to keep them because of their special diets. Australians are working hard to solve these problems. Time is important for koalas, as it is for all animals in danger.

GLOSSARY / INDEX

Arboreal: adapted for living or moving about in trees (page 9)

Endangered species: animals whose numbers are getting so low they might not survive. These animals face extinction. (page 29)

Extinct: ceasing to exist, no longer living (page 6)

Fuse-joined: two fingers are permanently bonded into one (page 10)

Incisor: sharp-edged front teeth, used to cut and gnaw (page 10)

Marsupials: animals whose young finish growing in a pouch or pocket on the mother's abdomen (page 6)

Molars: teeth in the back of the jaw with a broad surface for grinding (page 10)

Pouched animals: those with a pocket or bag on the abdomen in which to carry a small baby (page 6)

Predators: animals who hunt and kill another animal for food (page 5)

Prehistoric time: before events were written down as recorded history (page 5)

Species: animals that are alike and can reproduce among themselves but not with another species (page 6)

Teat: the nipple from which a baby nurses to get its mother's milk (page 21)